D0167826

Love to create amazing stories? Good, because this one stars YOU. Get ready to laugh with all your friends—you can play with as many people as you want! Make sure to keep this book on your shelf. You'll want to read it again and again!

Are You Ready to Laugh?

- One person picks a story—you can start at the beginning, the middle, or the end of the book.

- Ask a friend to call out a word that the space asks for—noun, verb, or something else—and write it in the blank space. If there's more than one person, ask the next person to say a word. Extra points for creativity!

- When all the spaces are filled in, you have your very own Funny Fill-In. Read it out loud for a laugh.

- Want to play by yourself? Just fold over the page and use the cardboard insert at the back as a writing pad. Fill in the blank parts of speech list, and copy your answers into the story.

Fun Fact! Make sure you check out the amazing **Fun Facts** that appear on every page!

To play the game, you'll need to know how to form sentences. This list with examples of the parts of speech and other terms will help you get started:

Noun: The name of a person, place, thing, or idea
   Examples: tree, mouth, creature
   *The **ocean** is full of colorful **fish**.*

Adjective: A word that describes a noun or pronoun
   Examples: green, lazy, friendly
   *My **silly** dog won't stop laughing!*

Verb: An action word. In the present tense, a verb often ends in –s or –ing. If the space asks for past tense, changing the vowel or adding a –d or –ed to the end usually will set the sentence in the past.
   Examples: swim, hide, plays, running (present tense); biked, rode, jumped (past tense)
   *The giraffe **skips** across the savanna.*
   *The flower **opened** after the rain.*

Adverb: A word that describes a verb and usually ends in –ly
   Examples: quickly, lazily, soundlessly
   *Kelley **greedily** ate all the carrots.*

Plural: More than one
   Examples: mice, telephones, wrenches
   *Why are all the **doors** closing?*

Silly Word or Exclamation: A funny sound, a made-up word, a word you think is totally weird, or a noise someone or something might make
   Examples: Ouch! No way! Foozleduzzle! Yikes!
   *"**Darn!**" shouted Jim. "These cupcakes are sour!"*

Specific Words: There are many more ways to make your story hilarious. When asked for something like a number, animal, or body part, write in something you think is especially funny.

- your name
  - your age
- your name
  - number
- country
  - exotic animal
- silly word
  - name beginning with "C"
- relative's name
  - breakfast food
- verb ending in –ing
  - verb ending in –ing
- your name
  - large number
- something small
  - something furry
- something green, plural
  - zodiac sign
- silly word

TOP SECRET

Fun Fact! THE U.S. CENTRAL INTELLIGENCE AGENCY ONCE STRAPPED CAMERAS ON PIGEONS TRAINED TO FLY OVER ENEMY TARGETS.

№ AGENT NGK-02

[YOUR NAME]

Agent _____ is _____ . (S)he is an asset of the Super Secret Spy Agency currently in training
        your name   your age

at the Super Secret Spy Academy. Agent _____ is fluent in _____ languages after growing up
                                          your name   number

in several countries, including Kenya, Thailand, Australia, and _____ . Good with animals, the
                                                                    country

agent keeps several exotic pets: Bert, a(n) _____ ; _____ , an iguana; and
                                               exotic animal   silly word

_____ , a camel. As a child in Kenya, (s)he had a "pet" giraffe that would stop by for
name beginning with "C"

breakfast every morning. It was named _____ and really loved _____ .
                                          relative's name   breakfast food

Agent excels at _____ and _____ . In his/her free time, Agent _____
                  verb ending in –ing   verb ending in –ing   your name

is a speedy reader, and has read over _____ books! Known fears are _____ and
                                          large number   something small

_____ . Known allergens are _____ . Agent is a _____ ,
something furry   something green, plural   zodiac sign

and therefore has traits perfect for a successful spy career. Agent's code name is: _____ .
                                                                                      silly word

- board game
  - sport
- noun
  - body part
- noun, plural
  - noun, plural
- noun
  - letter
- adjective
  - adjective
- type of vehicle
  - something scary
- verb ending in –ing
  - adjective
- friend's name
  - color
- shape
  - school subject
- noun, plural

Fun Fact! WASHINGTON, D.C., BECAME THE CAPITAL OF THE UNITED STATES IN 1790. A FRENCH ARTIST AND ENGINEER, PIERRE L'ENFANT, CAREFULLY PLANNED THE CITY.

IN THIS TEMPLE
AS IN THE HEARTS OF THE P...
FOR WHOM HE SAVED THE ...
THE MEMORY OF ABRAHAM LI...
IS ENSHRINED FOREVE...

NOT A SECRET DOOR TO
THE SUPER SECRET SPY ACADEMY

SUPER
SECRET
SPY
ACADE

Super Secret Spy Academy

I was recruited to the Super Secret Spy Academy because I am a _____ master and good at

(board game)

_____ . My school is hidden underneath the Lincoln Memorial in Washington, D.C., and can only

(sport)

be accessed by a secret _____ noun _____ under Abraham Lincoln's _____ . We have to be careful there

(noun)   (body part)

aren't any _____ watching when we go in! Sometimes I'm late because I have to wait around to

(noun, plural)

blend in with the _____ . I always bring a _____ , just in case. My teacher is Ms. _____ .

(noun, plural)   (noun)   (letter)

She's really _____ , but hates it when we're late. I have a pretty _____ class schedule.

(adjective)   (adjective)

This year I'm taking "Disguise & Camouflage," "_____ Driving," "_____-ology,"

(type of vehicle)   (something scary)

"Code Breaking," and "Stealthy _____ ." My school is _____ because my best

(verb ending in –ing)   (adjective)

friend _____ goes here too. (S)he has _____ hair, _____ glasses, and

(friend's name)   (color)   (shape)

is a _____ genius. When we're not busy learning spy craft, we like to ride our _____ .

(school subject)   (noun, plural)

- adjective ending in –est
  - adjective
- noun, plural
  - size
- adjective
  - friend's name
- adverb ending in –ly
  - fruit
- same fruit, plural
  - noun
- verb
  - verb
- something spooky
  - country
- number
  - same friend's name
- body part
  - something sparkly
- noun

Fun Fact!

THE **LIBRARY OF CONGRESS** HAS **838 MILES** (1,349 KM) OF SHELVES FILLED WITH **BOOKS!**

An Unexpected Mission

My class is on a field trip at the Library of Congress. We've been assigned research papers, so it's lucky that

we are visiting one of the world's _____ libraries. First we get a tour of the building;
                                    adjective ending in –est

it's _____ and very fancy. The shelves are filled with _____ and artifacts. There are
        adjective   noun, plural

_____ and _____ books displayed on stands. _____ gets in trouble for trying
    size   adjective   friend's name

to _____ eat a(n) _____ . "No _____ allowed near the _____ !"
   adverb ending in –ly   fruit   same fruit, plural   noun

yells a librarian. We _____ some books and sit down in a reading room to _____ on
                          verb   verb

our papers. Mine is on the _____ history of _____ . After _____
                           something spooky   country   number

minutes _____ and I are bored out of our _____ and decide to
        same friend's name   body part

explore. We see _____ on a _____ in a roped-off
                something sparkly   noun

area with a sign that says: "DO NOT ENTER."

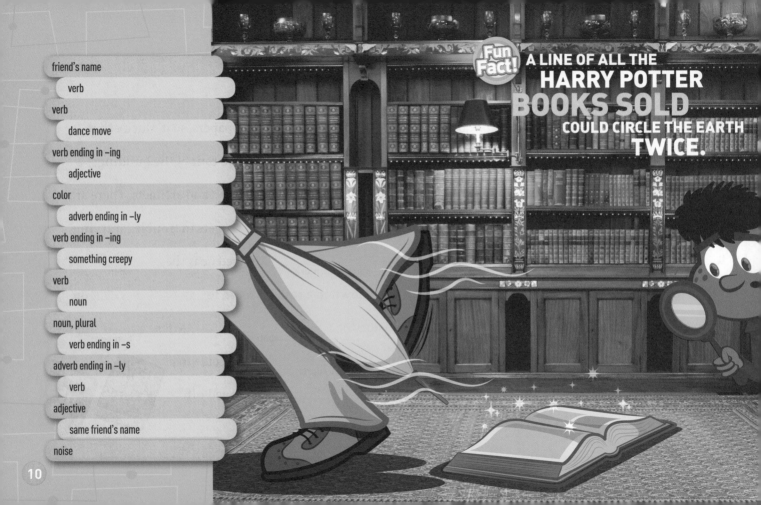

friend's name

    verb

verb

    dance move

verb ending in –ing

    adjective

color

    adverb ending in –ly

verb ending in –ing

    something creepy

verb

    noun

noun, plural

    verb ending in –s

adverb ending in –ly

    verb

adjective

    same friend's name

noise

Fun Fact! A LINE OF ALL THE **HARRY POTTER BOOKS SOLD** COULD CIRCLE THE EARTH **TWICE.**

The Mysterious Man

_____ and I _____ the sign that says "DO NOT ENTER." We _____ over the
friend's name _____ _verb_ _____ _verb_

rope and _____ into the restricted section. We're having fun _____ when I
_____ _dance move_ _____ _verb ending in –ing_

notice a(n) _____ man wearing a trench coat and a _____ hat. He's carrying an umbrella
_____ _adjective_ _____ _color_

and behaving _____ . My spy senses start _____ . I follow him into a hidden
_____ _adverb ending in –ly_ _____ _verb ending in –ing_

room. He's taking pictures with a camera that looks like a _____ ! I _____ him from
_____ _something creepy_ _____ _verb_

between a(n) _____ and some _____ . I'm stealthy, so he doesn't notice me. The man
_____ _noun_ _____ _noun, plural_

_____ books and _____ throws them on the floor. He's searching for
verb ending in –s _____ _adverb ending in –ly_

something. When he moves to the next row, I _____ at one of the _____ books he
_____ _verb_ _____ _adjective_

discarded. "HEY, I FOUND YOU!" _____ shouts, entering the room. The door shuts
_____ _same friend's name_

with a _____ . I jump up, but the stranger is already gone.
_____ _noise_

science topic

    verb ending in –s

adjective

    something sharp

verb ending in –ing

    verb ending in –s

something expensive

    noun, plural

something enormous

    exclamation

feeling

    science lab equipment

body part

    adjective

something tiny

    color

item of clothing

Fun Fact! IF YOU SPENT ONE DOLLAR EVERY SECOND, IT WOULD TAKE ABOUT **32 YEARS** TO SPEND A BILLION DOLLARS.

The Theft!

At school, during _____ class, Ms. B _____ into the room.
science topic   verb ending in –s

She's the _____ director of our school and is about as friendly as a(n) _____ .
adjective   something sharp

Ms. B tells us that a book was stolen from the Library of Congress while our class was _____
verb ending in –ing

there. She _____ that this book is worth more than _____ ,
verb ending in –s   something expensive

because it contains the _____ to the vault at the Federal Reserve Bank in New York City.
noun, plural

This vault contains enough gold to equal a(n) _____ . _____ ! I want
something enormous   exclamation

to tell Ms. B what I saw, but I'm _____ to admit I was in the restricted section. I remove my
feeling

_____ and shakily raise my _____ . I tell my story about the
science lab equipment   body part

_____ man in the hat in a voice the size of a(n) _____ . "YOU DID WHAT?!"
adjective   something tiny

shouts Ms. B, turning as _____ as her itchy-looking _____ .
color   item of clothing

adjective

   noun, plural

adjective

   color

friend's name (male)

   friend's name (female)

verb ending in –ed

   animal

continent

   noun, plural

item of clothing

   historical figure

color

   adjective

Fun Fact! YOUR EYES PROCESS MORE THAN **120 MILLION** BITS OF INFORMATION EVERY SECOND.

Two agents arrive at the Academy to help. Agent M is _____ and is wearing dark _____ .

adjective   noun, plural

Agent H is very _____ and has vibrant _____ hair, which might be a wig. I look closer and

adjective   color

realize the agents are _____ and _____ . My friends are real spies!

friend's name (male)   friend's name (female)

I'm _____ to the case. We return to the scene of the crime—the restricted section

verb ending in –ed

at the Library of Congress. Books are everywhere, piled as high as a(n) _____ , with titles like

animal

the *Treasure Map of* _____ . But someone re-shelved all the _____ that were

continent   noun, plural

on the floor earlier, and there's no sign of the man with the _____ . Discouraged, we leave,

item of clothing

and we stand outside by a statue of _____ . On the statue's head is a hat—

historical figure

the same _____ one that the _____ man from the library wore! Our first clue!

color   adjective

- relative's name
- silly word
- adjective
- adjective
- liquid
- number
- type of fruit
- body part
- verb
- vehicle
- royal title
- silly word
- verb
- electronic gadget
- shape
- color
- something really old
- noun

Fun Fact! IN 1900, THE WORLD'S LARGEST CITY WAS LONDON, ENGLAND.

Hat Shop Hoax

The hat we found at the Library of Congress has a tag that says " _____ and _____ —
<u>relative's name</u>   <u>silly word</u>

Purveyor of _____ Hats." It's a hat shop in England. So Agent M, Agent H, and I catch a flight to
<u>adjective</u>

London to look for a(n) _____ man. We fly first-class, and the attendants bring me _____
<u>adjective</u>   <u>liquid</u>

perfectly chilled to _____ degrees. They also bring fresh _____ to put on my
<u>number</u>   <u>type of fruit</u>

_____ to help me _____ . I could get used to this! We get off the plane, hop in
<u>body part</u>   <u>verb</u>

a(n) _____ , and head to Baker Street, the location of the hat shop and home of famous
<u>vehicle</u>

detective _____ _____ . I _____ with my _____
<u>royal title</u>   <u>silly word</u>   <u>verb</u>   <u>electronic gadget</u>

around the store. Near a table filled with _____ and _____ hats, I see a familiar book.
<u>shape</u>   <u>color</u>

It looks older than _____ . Then I notice a trench coat and umbrella hanging on a
<u>something really old</u>

_____ ! The mysterious man must be here!
<u>noun</u>

- verb
  - verb
- adverb ending in –ly
  - color
- something soft
  - sound
- verb ending in –ing
  - body part, plural
- something hard
  - noun
- adjective
  - animal
- item of clothing
  - verb
- adjective
  - adjective
- verb ending in –s
  - adjective
- adjective

Fun Fact! THE ORIGINAL UNIFORMS FOR UMPIRES IN MAJOR LEAGUE BASEBALL INCLUDED TOP HATS!

The Speedy Exit

I know the thief we've been looking for is in this hat shop! I have to _____ the other spies!
_{verb}

But I _____ _____ and knock over a rack of _____ and
_{verb} _{adverb ending in –ly} _{color}

_____ hats. It lands with a huge _____ . The shopkeeper comes
_{something soft} _{sound}

_____ into the room, with the other agents close on his _____ .
_{verb ending in –ing} _{body part, plural}

Agent H is furious—her stare could cut a(n) _____ . "Please excuse my _____,"
_{something hard} _{noun}

she says. "(S)he's just a very _____ _____ ." Agent M grabs
_{adjective} _{animal}

my _____ and tries to _____ me out of the _____
_{item of clothing} _{verb} _{adjective}

room. But now I see the shopkeeper's _____ face up close. It's him! The thief is the
_{adjective}

shopkeeper! Agent H _____ to the shopkeeper for my _____
_{verb ending in –s} _{adjective}

behavior. We make a(n) _____ exit so we don't blow our cover.
_{adjective}

- noun
  - verb
- verb
  - noun
- dance move
  - body part, plural
- number
  - noun
- verb
  - noun
- adjective
  - animal print
- color
  - verb ending in –ing
- electronic gadget
  - verb
- small number

Fun Fact! THE LONDON BRIDGE THAT KEPT FALLING DOWN IS NOW IN ARIZONA, IN THE UNITED STATES.

An Unexpected Holiday

I'm in big _____ . The agents won't _____ to me; I almost blew our cover.
noun · *verb*

But I _____ : "The book thief is the shopkeeper, and he's just down the _____ !"
verb · *noun*

I _____ to the store. Agent H catches up quickly—she has long _____ .
dance move · *body part, plural*

We weren't even _____ blocks away, but by the time we get to the shop there's a sign on the front
number

_____ that says "ON HOLIDAY—Back Next Week." We _____ back through a park.
noun · *verb*

I scan the _____ for the thief. I see a(n) _____ lady wearing _____ pants,
noun · *adjective* · *animal print*

a crazily patterned shirt, and a(n) _____ striped hat. "I saw you earlier," she says. "The hatmaker's
color

gone to Paris. If you're _____ for him, he was hurrying to the next train." I do a quick
verb ending in –ing

check on my spy _____ and confirm that we need to _____ to
electronic gadget · *verb*

London St. Pancras station. We only have _____ minutes!
small number

- verb
  - color
- noun
  - adjective
- something shiny
  - electronic gadget, plural
- verb ending in –s
  - number
- celebrity
  - verb ending in –s
- adjective
  - direction
- verb
  - speed
- body part
  - verb
- noun
  - silly word
- noun

Fun Fact!

A VILLAGE IN **SOMERSET, ENGLAND,** TURNED ITS RED **TELEPHONE BOOTH** INTO A TINY LIBRARY.

TELEPHONE

The Crazy Televator

We're short on time to _____ (verb) the train and the thief, but spies always know a shortcut. We reach

a(n) _____ (color) phone booth with grimy windows. It looks small from the outside, but when we open

the _____ (noun) it's a(n) _____ (adjective) elevator! It has lots of _____ (something shiny) buttons

and weird _____ (electronic gadget, plural) . Agent M _____ (verb ending in –s) a _____ (number) -digit code. Then a light

turns on and _____ (celebrity) says, "Welcome to the Televator. Destination, please." Agent H

_____ (verb ending in –s) the Televator to St. Pancras train station and we're off! It is not a(n) _____ (adjective)

elevator—we go _____ (direction) and then _____ (verb) right. We must be going _____ (speed) !

I'm dizzy and my _____ (body part) hurts; I'm definitely ready to get off the Televator. Finally, we

_____ (verb) to a stop and the _____ (noun) bangs open. We're in the train station with just moments

to spare. " _____ (silly word) ," the elevator says. We get to the train just as the _____ (noun) blows.

adjective

    color

gemstone, plural

    noun

celebrity

    language

liquid

    adjective

big number

    adjective

type of metal

    number

vegetable

    type of seafood

type of cheese

    electronic gadget

flavor

    type of candy

favorite food

Fun Fact!

TAKING A TRAIN
1,000 MILES (1,609 KM)
PRODUCES LESS THAN HALF THE
CARBON EMISSIONS
PRODUCED BY TRAVELING THE SAME
ROUTE BY PLANE.

Delicious Dining Car

After a run-in with our thief and a(n) _____ Televator ride, I'm starving. So we all head to the
adjective

dining car. It's amazing! The waiters wear _____ uniforms with coordinating _____ .
color   gemstone, plural

Every table has its own chandelier and a personal _____ . Our waiter's name is _____ ,
noun   celebrity

and (s)he only speaks _____ . I order _____ , but (s)he thinks I want super-_____ size!
language   liquid   adjective

(S)he brings us _____ orders. That's far too much, so we share with the _____ tables. Next (s)he
big number   adjective

brings a(n) _____ tray of _____ sandwiches. I try a(n) _____ sandwich,
type of metal   number   vegetable

a(n) _____ sandwich, and a(n) _____ sandwich. I made sure they weren't
type of seafood   type of cheese

dangerous by testing them with my spy _____ . The dessert trolley comes and we make
electronic gadget

_____ and _____ sundaes. Agent M likes sprinkles on his, I like _____ ,
flavor   type of candy   favorite food

but Agent H doesn't even like ice cream. We're so full that we go back to our seats and take a nap.

adjective

   adjective

verb

   body part

verb ending in –ing

   adjective

adverb ending in –ly

   verb ending in –ing

number

   type of material

noun

   verb

noun

   verb ending in –ed

color

   type of dog, plural

language

   noun, plural

Fun Fact! THE FIRST MODERN **HIGH-SPEED** TRAIN WAS CALLED THE "BULLET TRAIN."

Caught on the Platform

After our _____ meal and a(n) _____ nap, we arrive at the Gare du Nord in Paris.
            adjective   adjective

I really want to _____ my _____ . I'm _____ under the
                    verb   body part   verb ending in –ing

_____ rack, so my head is bent _____ . As I'm _____ out of the
    adjective   adverb ending in –ly   verb ending in –ing

train, I see him! _____ train cars ahead of us, the book thief is wearing his trench coat and carrying
                    number

an umbrella and a(n) _____ briefcase. I use my special spy _____ to jump
                          type of material   noun

over seats and eventually _____ through the _____ of the train. I fall to the platform
                              verb   noun

and suddenly get _____ in the leashes of two _____ _____ .
                    verb ending in –ed   color   type of dog, plural

Their owner yells at me in _____ until I can get away. The book thief is now gone.
                              language

But I'm so focused on catching up that I run into a stack of _____ that topples onto
                                                                noun, plural

our whole spy team!

adjective

vehicle

verb

adjective

verb

noun

verb

type of appliance

color

item of clothing

famous painting

monument

type of hat

type of bread

type of cheese

something gross

insect

noun

Fun Fact! FRENCH FRIES CAME FROM BELGIUM, NOT FRANCE.

Sightseeing Paris Style

In the _____ terminal, I see the book thief getting in a(n) _____ !
    adjective   vehicle

We _____ to catch it, but it drives away. We've lost him. The agents and I call HQ to get
       verb

_____ orders and any new intel. We're told to stay put just in case we _____
  adjective   verb

the thief again. We pass the _____ by sightseeing. We rent bicycles and _____
                                  noun   verb

the city. I have a special _____ that I modify to pedal for me! We stop and Agent M
                            type of appliance

buys a _____ _____ . Agent H buys a copy of _____ . I buy a
        color   item of clothing   famous painting

keychain of _____ and a _____ . We eat a lunch of _____ and
              monument   type of hat   type of bread

_____ in a park. We get _____ too, because it's a French specialty, but I
  type of cheese   something gross

think I'd rather eat a(n) _____ . But we're having a blast! We realize we have
                             insect

time to see the main _____ —the Eiffel Tower.
                         noun

29

- adjective
  - verb, past tense
- verb
  - adjective
- big number
  - verb
- adjective
  - verb
- adjective
  - verb
- sport
  - animal
- noun
  - color
- verb ending in –ing
  - adverb ending in –ly
- verb ending in –s
  - adjective
- adjective

Fun Fact! SPECIAL SATELLITES CAN SEE A GRAPEFRUIT SITTING ON A PICNIC TABLE FROM 250 MILES (400 KM) ABOVE EARTH.

On Top of the Eiffel Tower

The Eiffel Tower is so _____ (adjective) . We still haven't heard from Super Secret Spy HQ

or _____ (verb, past tense) the book thief. So we _____ (verb) the stairs to the top. _____ (adjective)

choice; there must be _____ (big number) of them! Once we get to the top, Agent M and Agent H need to

_____ (verb) down because they're _____ (adjective) . So I use the spy binoculars to _____ (verb) the view.

The sunset is _____ (adjective) , and I watch all the Parisian people _____ (verb) in the grass.

There are children playing _____ (sport) , a(n) _____ (animal) with a(n) _____ (noun) ,

and a man sitting on a _____ (color) bench. Wait! It's the thief we've been _____ (verb ending in –ing) for!

I watch as a woman wearing a beret sits and _____ (adverb ending in –ly) hands him a note. The book thief

_____ (verb ending in –s) the note, crumples it, and drops it into a(n) _____ (adjective) garbage can as he

walks away. I've got to go get it—that note could be _____ (adjective) to our mission!

- verb ending in –ing
  - body part, plural
- adjective
  - verb
- spy gadget
  - verb
- something sticky
  - something blue
- adjective
  - food
- store
  - electronic gadget
- sound
  - verb ending in –s
- verb ending in –ing
  - same electronic gadget

Fun Fact!

A MAN ONCE **RODE A BIKE** DOWN THE EIFFEL TOWER'S **1,665 STEPS.**

The Note and the Code

I'm _____ (verb ending in –ing) down the stairs of the Eiffel Tower before the other agents can even get on

their _____ (body part, plural) . I'm fast and _____ (adjective) , so I can _____ (verb) easily through

the crowd. But by the time I get to the bench, the book thief and the lady are gone. Agent H uses her

_____ (spy gadget) to scan the area, in case they're still nearby. I have to dig to _____ (verb) the note

from the garbage can; it's covered up by _____ (something sticky) , _____ (something blue) , and

several pieces of _____ (adjective) _____ (food) . I finally find the note; it's written in code on the

back of a(n) _____ (store) receipt. I begin to decipher the code with my _____ (electronic gadget) .

It makes a(n) _____ (sound) as it _____ (verb ending in –s) each symbol. Agent M finally arrives,

huffing and _____ (verb ending in –ing) . Just then, the _____ (same electronic gadget) cracks the code! It's an

address, and our next destination is Spain.

33

- verb ending in –ing
  - verb
- body part, plural
  - liquid
- noun, plural
  - vegetable, plural
- adjective
  - body part
- verb ending in –s
  - item of clothing
- verb ending in –ing
  - animal
- noun
  - number
- vegetable, plural
  - verb ending in –ing
- something sticky

Fun Fact! THERE ARE MORE THAN **10,000** KINDS OF TOMATOES. SOME CAN WEIGH MORE THAN **THREE POUNDS** (1.4 KG)!

The agents and I are _____ at the open door of an airplane. I'm nervous, but there's no other
                        verb ending in –ing

way to get out. We jump, _____ our parachute cords, and land on the ground in Buñol, Spain. I look
                          verb

down and my _____ are in a puddle of red _____ . We need to get across town,
             body part, plural   liquid

but there are _____ everywhere. And everyone is throwing _____ at each other!
              noun, plural   vegetable, plural

A(n) _____ one comes whizzing by and hits Agent M square in the _____ . Another
     adjective   body part

one _____ on my favorite _____ . I learned at Super Secret Spy Academy to
    verb ending in –s   item of clothing

blend in by _____ like a(n) _____ . I know we'll get across _____ faster
            verb ending in –ing   animal   noun

if we do that and join the fight. We each grab _____ _____ and start _____
                                               number   vegetable, plural   verb ending in –ing

and running. Eventually, covered in dripping _____ , we arrive at our destination.
                                             something sticky

35

adjective

    color

noise

    noun

animal

    adverb ending in –ly

number

    noun

vegetable, plural

    adjective

verb ending in –ing

    noun

item of clothing, plural

    something soft, plural

type of bird, plural

    verb

verb

    noun

Fun Fact! THE SPORT OF PARKOUR— MOVING OVER OBSTACLES— WAS DEVELOPED IN THE **SUBURBS OF PARIS** IN THE 1980s.

At the address from the decoded note, we find a(n) _____ _____ house.
adjective   color

I hear a(n) _____ , and a(n) _____ comes flying off the roof and lands on the street
noise   noun

in front of us. We look up, and I'm expecting to see a(n) _____ , but it's the book thief! He jumps
animal

_____ from one roof to another and he's quickly getting away. _____ houses down
adverb ending in –ly   number

there's a(n) _____ that I can climb to the roof. I'm still covered in _____
noun   vegetable, plural

and the roof is _____ , so I keep _____ around. I jump to the next
adjective   verb ending in –ing

roof and have to grab the _____ so I don't fall off. I run through a clothesline filled with
noun

_____ and _____ and lose sight of the thief. Suddenly,
item of clothing, plural   something soft, plural

a flock of _____ flies toward me and I have to _____ . When the air
type of bird, plural   verb

clears, I see the book thief _____ off the roof, down to the _____ .
verb   noun

- verb
  - item of clothing
- verb
  - verb ending in –ing
- body part
  - adjective
- noise
  - color
- material
  - noun, plural
- adjective
  - verb ending in –s
- verb
  - verb ending in –s
- vehicle
  - verb
- adjective
  - verb

Fun Fact! THE OLDEST RESTAURANT IN THE WORLD IS IN MADRID, SPAIN, AND HAS BEEN OPEN SINCE 1725.

I'm stuck on the roof. I _____ (verb) back to the clothesline, grab a(n) _____ (item of clothing), and use

the power line to _____ (verb) down to the street. I'm _____ (verb ending in –ing) through the air, out of control,

but I see the thief! I stick my _____ (body part) out and trip him; we both crash into a(n) _____ (adjective)

outdoor café. There's an enormous _____ (noise), and _____ (color) tables and _____ (material)

_____ (noun, plural) go flying. As the thief scrambles to his feet, the _____ (adjective) book _____ (verb ending in –s)

out of his briefcase. I _____ (verb) the book, but the thief _____ (verb ending in –s) through the café. Just then

the agents show up in a(n) _____ (vehicle). They help me up, and we _____ (verb) the book together,

hoping that the plans are still in it. The pages are _____ (adjective) and hard to read,

but we _____ (verb) the plans to the vault and know that the gold will

be safe. Mission accomplished!

- number
  - color
- verb
  - verb ending in –ing
- ocean creature, plural
  - flavor
- noun
  - verb
- adverb ending in –ly
  - verb
- something hot
  - something red
- item of clothing
  - something soft
- verb ending in –ing
  - adverb ending in –ly
- verb
  - verb
- vehicle

Fun Fact!

THERE ARE
SEVEN QUINTILLION,
FIVE HUNDRED QUADRILLION
GRAINS OF SAND
ON EARTH.

Wacky Beach Tan

After all our spy adventures, we're exhausted. Our flight is not for _____ hours, and we're near the
                                                                    number

coast, so we decide to hit the beach. The water is a beautiful _____ and we _____
                                                                    color   verb

right in. After _____ and playing with some _____ , we get some
                  verb ending in –ing   ocean creature, plural

_____ ice cream. Well, everyone except for Agent H—she's not a _____ .
   flavor   noun

We _____ in the sun and _____ become tired. We must have all fallen asleep,
     verb   adverb ending in –ly

because hours later I _____ up. My skin feels like _____ . I look down
                        verb   something hot

and I'm the color of a(n) _____ ! I'm sunburnt and have strange lines from my
                             something red

_____ and _____ . "Oh no!" shouts Agent H. "We're _____
   item of clothing   something soft   verb ending in –ing

to miss our flight!" We _____ collect our things and _____ across the scorching
                          adverb ending in –ly   verb

sand. We _____ into the first _____ we can find.
            verb   vehicle

exclamation
- small number

verb
- vehicle

color
- same vehicle

verb ending in –ing
- noun

verb
- animal

body part, plural
- relative's name

weird job, plural
- piece of clothing, plural

body part, plural
- number

number
- verb

Fun Fact! THE HUMAN BODY CONTAINS A TINY AMOUNT OF GOLD.

The Vault

"_____ ! Our flight is in _____ minutes!" I _____ . "No problem!"
    exclamation   small number   verb

says our _____ driver. He pushes a _____ button on the dashboard. The _____
       vehicle   color   same vehicle

takes off, and it feels like we're _____ ! We get to the _____ with time to spare, and
                 verb ending in –ing   noun

_____ all the way home. Per orders from HQ, we must take the book to the vault in New York City
  verb

faster than a(n) _____ . When we get there, a machine scans our _____ before
           animal   body part, plural

we can enter the vault. It's deep underground and smells like _____ . The _____
               relative's name   weird job, plural

have to wear special _____ to protect their _____ from the gold.
       piece of clothing, plural   body part, plural

We watch them place the book in the vault with the gold. It takes _____ guards to shut the door, and
               number

_____ more to _____ the lock. Now that's security every spy can admire!
  number   verb

adjective

    verb

verb ending in –s

    adjective

noun

    feeling

verb

    noun, plural

adverb ending in –ly

    verb ending in –ed

huge number

    noun

animal

    noun

verb

    noun, plural

adjective

Fun Fact! **FINGERPRINTS CAN LAST FOR UP TO 40 YEARS ON PAPER.**

After ensuring the _____ book is locked safely in the vault, the agents and I _____

adjective · verb

back home to Washington, D.C. At the Super Secret Spy HQ, Ms. B debriefs us. She _____ us for

verb ending in –s

a(n) _____ job and tells us that the _____ we brought back will be examined by the

adjective · noun

_____ team. Already, they _____ that the book thief is none other than the

feeling · verb

nefarious supervillian J.A.B. The _____ we found will help the agency know more about him.

noun, plural

Most _____ , we _____ his attempt to steal _____ dollars.

adverb ending in –ly · verb ending in –ed · huge number

The agents and I each have to fill out a pile of _____ taller than a(n) _____ and

noun · animal

take _____-detector tests. We're given one day to _____ and recover, and then we're

noun · verb

expected back at our _____ . After returning to the Super Secret Spy Academy, I'm awarded a

noun, plural

Gold Star for _____ service.

adjective

adjective

    relative's name

verb, present tense

    noun, plural

famous spy character

    historical figure

adjective

    electronic gadget

adjective

    noun, plural

friend's name

    type of toy

noun

    noun

noun

    your name

noun

    continent

Fun Fact! CAMP PEARY IS THOUGHT TO BE THE SPY SCHOOL FOR THE CIA.

Mission: Super Spy

My spy adventure was crazy and _____ . I have so many stories to tell _____ .
adjective   relative's name

Sometimes I _____ some small _____ and the stories are even better, just like
verb, present tense   noun, plural

I'm _____ ! But now that I'm back, I have so much homework to do. I have a paper
famous spy character

about _____ and a presentation about the _____ benefits of _____ .
historical figure   adjective   electronic gadget

Besides that, it's _____ to be home and see my family, _____ , and pets. _____
adjective   noun, plural   friend's name

just bought a new _____ , so we're learning how to use it. One day after school, I'm
type of toy

working in my _____ when my handheld _____ beeps an urgent message. I use my
noun   noun

spy _____ to call HQ. Ms. B answers: "Agent _____ , we need your help," she says.
noun   your name

"Agents H and M will join you. This is an all-hands situation. There are strange _____ signals coming
noun

from _____ , and J.A.B. is still on the loose!" My next mission has just begun!
continent

Credits

Cover: (RT CTR), Volodymyrkrasyuk/Dreamstime; (UP RT), Cbenjasuwan/Dreamstime; (CTR), Dirk Ercken/Shutterstock; (LO LE), Andrei Shumskiy/Shutterstock; (LO RT), Vitaly Korovin/Shutterstock; 4 (background), Sergiy Serdyuk/Alamy; 4 (RT CTR), Annette Shaff/Shutterstock; 4 (LO RT), LeonP/Shutterstock; 6, fstockfoto/Dreamstime; 8, Lester Lefkowitz/Getty Images; 10, photogl/iStockphoto; 12, Chris Barrett/Hedrich Blessing/Arcaid/Corbis; 14, Pierdelune/iStockphoto; 16, Richard Allen/Alamy; 18, Neil Setchfield/Alamy; 20, I Love Images/Corbis; 22, Peter Crome/Alamy; 24, Sam Tinson/Rex USA; 26, Brotch Images/Alamy; 28, Tomas Marek/Dreamstime; 30, Rodd Halstead/Getty Images; 32, BremecR/iStockphoto; 34, Jasper Juinen/Getty Images; 36, Rtsubin/Dreamstime; 38, Clicks/Getty Images; 40, Gallo Images/Getty Images; 42, Edward J Bock III/Dreamstime; 44, mbbirdy/iStockphoto; 46, Barbara Helgason/Dreamstime

---

Published by the National Geographic Society

John M. Fahey, *Chairman of the Board and Chief Executive Officer*
Declan Moore, *Executive Vice President; President, Publishing and Travel*
Melina Gerosa Bellows, *Executive Vice President; Chief Creative Officer, Books, Kids, and Family*

Prepared by the Book Division

Hector Sierra, *Senior Vice President and General Manager*
Nancy Laties Feresten, *Senior Vice President, Kids Publishing and Media*
Jay Sumner, *Director of Photography, Children's Publishing*
Jennifer Emmett, *Vice President, Editorial Director, Children's Books*
Eva Absher-Schantz, *Design Director, Kids Publishing and Media*
R. Gary Colbert, *Production Director*
Jennifer A. Thornton, *Director of Managing Editorial*

Staff for This Book

Kate Olesin, *Project Editor*
James Hiscott Jr., *Art Director*

Kelley Miller, *Senior Photo Editor*
Ruth Ann Thompson, *Designer*
Ariane Szu-Tu, *Editorial Assistant*
Callie Broaddus, *Design Production Assistant*
Margaret Leist, *Illustrations Assistant*
Ruth Musgrave, *Writer*
Jason Tharp, *Illustrator*
Bri Bertoia, *Freelance Photo Editor*
Grace Hill, *Associate Managing Editor*
Joan Gossett, *Production Editor*
Lewis R. Bassford, *Production Manager*
Susan Borke, *Legal and Business Affairs*

Production Services

Phillip L. Schlosser, *Senior Vice President*
Chris Brown, *Vice President, NG Book Manufacturing*
George Bounelis, *Vice President, Production Services*
Nicole Elliott, *Manager*
Rachel Faulise, *Manager*
Robert L. Barr, *Manager*

CELEBRATING 125 YEARS

The National Geographic Society is one of the world's largest nonprofit scientific and educational organizations. Founded in 1888 to "increase and diffuse geographic knowledge," the Society's mission is to inspire people to care about the planet. It reaches more than 400 million people worldwide each month through its official journal, *National Geographic*, and other magazines; National Geographic Channel; television documentaries; music; radio; films; books; DVDs; maps; exhibitions; live events; school publishing programs; interactive media; and merchandise. National Geographic has funded more than 10,000 scientific research, conservation, and exploration projects and supports an education program promoting geographic literacy.

For more information, please call 1-800-NGS LINE (647-5463) or write to the following address:

National Geographic Society, 1145 17th Street N.W., Washington, D.C. 20036-4688 U.S.A.

Visit us online at www.nationalgeographic.com/books

For librarians and teachers: www.ngchildrensbooks.org

More for kids from National Geographic: kids.nationalgeographic.com

For information about special discounts for bulk purchases, please contact National Geographic Books Special Sales: ngspecsales@ngs.org

For rights or permissions inquiries, please contact National Geographic Books Subsidiary Rights: ngbookrights@ngs.org

Copyright © 2013 National Geographic Society

All rights reserved. Reproduction of the whole or any part of the contents without written permission from the publisher is prohibited.

ISBN: 978-1-4263-1644-9

Printed in Hong Kong

13/THK/1